Scripture Text:
All Scripture quotations in this publication are from
the Holy Bible, New International Version.
Copyright © 1973, 1978, 1984, International Bible Society.

Additional Text:
Bill and Betty Howse
© 1986, World Home Bible League
South Holland, IL U.S.A.

Photographs: —Jim Whitmer

Published by

THE BIBLE LEAGUE

South Holland, Illinois 60473, USA
Burlington, Ontario, L7R 3Y8, Canada
Penrith, NSW 2751, Australia
Mt. Albert, New Zealand
Printed in U.S.A.
A100-32

Promises for Fathers

The responsibilities
of fatherhood
can be
joyous,
perplexing, and yes,
even overwhelming
at times!

However,
for the father who is
a child of God,
it is a task
that does not have to be
tackled alone.

Here are some promises
you as a father
may claim
from the Word of God . . .
from your Heavenly Father—
with love!

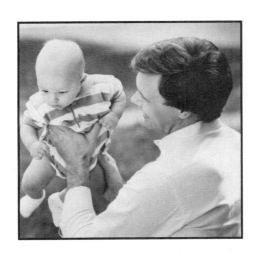

How great is the love
*   the Father*
*   has lavished on us,*
* that we should be called*
*   children of God!*
And that is what we are!

*   —1 John 3:1a*

Marriage

Marriage . . .
>How much effort it requires,
>>but then,
>>>how rewarding it can be!

Marriage . . .
>A part of God's plan
>>from the very beginning!

Marriage . . .
>A commitment that stands firm
>>through changes in life situations,
>>developing personalities,
>>and many temptations.

Marriage . . .
>So much effort—
>>so many rewards!

Answering some questions one day,
    Jesus said,
    "Haven't you read that
        at the beginning
        the Creator
            'made them male and female,'
        and said,
            'For this reason
                a man will leave
                his father and mother
                and be united to his wife,
                and the two will become
                    one flesh'?
    So they are no longer two,
        but one.
    Therefore
        what God has joined together,
            let man not separate."

                        —Matthew 19:4-6

Enjoy life with your wife,
    whom you love!

                        —Ecclesiastes 9:9a

May your fountain be blessed,
and may you rejoice
in the wife of your youth.

—Proverbs 5:18

Beginnings

Marriage is a time of beginning.

Another time of beginning
     in a marriage
    is the birth of a child.

. . . A dramatic,
    miraculous
      beginning!

And what pride, joy, and love
    a father feels
      as this tiny, new person
      is placed in his arms
      for the very first time!

For the child,
    it is a start
      into new surroundings—
      a brand new environment.

For the father,
    it is an untested start
      into this thing
      called parenting.

Joy and pride
mix with fear and uncertainty
      as new roles and responsibilities
      are cautiously approached.

Truly . . . a dramatic,
    miraculous
        beginning!

Sons are a heritage from the LORD,
     children a reward from him.
Like arrows in the hands of a warrior
     are sons born in one's youth.
Blessed is the man
     whose quiver is full of them.

—Psalm 127:3-5

Parenting

Miraculous and precious, indeed,
    is God's gift
        of a new, cuddly cherub
            in your home!

But . . .
    a complete change in lifestyle
        may come about for you as a father.

Your previously enjoyed
    tranquil night's sleep
        may be abruptly interrupted.
How often the "bottle cry"
    is sounded during
    the wee hours of the morning!

Other infant discomforts
    take their toll—
        not only of your night's rest
        but your waking hours as well.

Cradling the distressed baby
        in your strong arms,
    comforting with a soothing voice
        and gentle touch,
    will pave the way
        to stronger parental ties
            with your child
            in later years.

Indulge your child with affection . . .
    babies thrive
        on their parents' lavish love.

Grasp each fleeting opportunity!

The Father of compassion
and the God of all comfort, . . .
comforts us in all our troubles,
so that we can comfort
those in any trouble
with the comfort we ourselves
have received from God.

—2 Corinthians 1:3,4

The LORD your God, . . .
is gracious and compassionate,
slow to anger
and abounding in love.

—Joel 2:13

Role Confusion

We live in a changing society—
    technologically . . .
        morally.

The role expectations for fathers
    are quite different today
        than in grandfather's day!

House husband?
    Chances are
        your grandfather
            never heard of such a thing.

New rules for the game of life?

No! Our Creator's precepts for life
    are changeless.

So . . . where do you go for
    instruction . . .
        guidance . . .
            support?

Where can you find unchanging standard
    for this increasingly complicated
        role of fatherhood?

Try your own Heavenly Father!

Because of his infinite love
        for his own children,
    his Word will instruct you,
    his example will guide you, and
    his love will support you.

Stand firmly on the unchanging
    Word of God!

Do not be carried away
  by all kinds
    of strange teachings.

—*Hebrews 13:9*

"I the LORD
  do not change."

—*Malachi 3:6*

Your word, O LORD,
    is eternal;
  it stands firm
    in the heavens.

Your laws endure
    to this day,
  for all things serve you.

. . . I will ponder your statutes.

Your statutes are wonderful;
  therefore I obey them.

The entrance of your words
    gives light;
  it gives understanding
    to the simple.

—*Psalm 119:89, 91, 95,*
    129, 130

Fatherhood Responsibilities

"Dada." Music to your ears!
What a wonderful word
for your baby to say.

Dada . . .
Daddy . . .
Dad . . .
Father.

What an awesome responsibility
fatherhood is—
to be entrusted
with the care
of a precious, growing child.

And . . .
No aspect of that responsibility
is more important
than the spiritual nurturing
of your child.

In a world of harsh realities,
limitless dangers,
and uncounted temptations,
you may very well be
the only path
your child has
that leads to God.

Dada . . . Daddy . . . Dad . . . Father.

To be a godly father
to that growing child:
What an awesome responsibility!

Love the LORD your God
*   with all your heart and*
*   with all your soul and*
*   with all your strength.*

These commandments
*   that I give you today*
*   are to be upon your hearts.*

Impress them on your children.

Talk about them
*   when you sit at home and*
*   when you walk along the road,*
*   when you lie down and*
*   when you get up.*

Tie them as symbols
*   on your hands*
*   and bind them*
*   on your foreheads.*

Write them on the doorframes
*   of your houses*
*   and on your gates.*

—Deuteronomy 6:5-9

Fathers,
*   do not exasperate*
*   your children;*
*   instead,*
*   bring them up*
*   in the training and instruction*
*   of the Lord.*

—Ephesians 6:4

Spiritual Leadership

A godly father?
How does one fulfill that role?
In the hustle and bustle
    of earning a living,
        priorities are often confused
            and misdirected.

Ideally, family members
    take their nourishment together—
        both physically
            and spiritually.

What better time is there
    to read God's Word together
    than after a satisfying meal?
Or . . . before the family retires?

What a heritage to have
        . . . a father who prays
            for the welfare of his family
            at mealtime!
        . . . a father who brings
            his family with him
            to the house of God
            on the day of worship!
        . . . a father willing to assume
            that role of leadership
            his Creator entrusted to him!

He who fears the LORD
  has a secure fortress
  and for his children
    it will be a refuge.

—Proverbs 14:26

Observe the Sabbath day
  by keeping it holy,
  as the LORD your God
    has commanded you.

—Deuteronomy 5:12

Let us not give up
  meeting together,
  as some are in the habit of doing.

—Hebrews 10:25

Tell the next generation
the praiseworthy deeds
of the LORD,
his power,
and the wonders he has done. . . .
so the next generation
would know them,
even the children
yet to be born,
and they in turn
would tell their children.
Then they would put
their trust in God
and would not forget his deeds
but would keep his commands.

—Psalm 78:4-7

Discipline

Every child
must sometimes be
disciplined
by his
earthly
or
Heavenly Father
in order that he may learn
self-control,
responsibility, and
accountability.

Love
is the key
to discipline.

So . . .
Discipline your child
in love
because you love him,
just as your
Heavenly Father
disciplines
you
because
he loves you!

Do not despise
        the LORD's discipline
    and do not despise his rebuke,
    because the LORD
        disciplines those he loves,
        as a father the son
          he delights in.

—Proverbs 3:11, 12

Our fathers disciplined us
    for a little while
        as they thought best;
but God disciplines us
    for our good,
        that we may share
        in his holiness.

No discipline seems pleasant
    at the time, but painful.
Later on, however,
    it produces a harvest
        of righteousness and peace
        for those who have been
            trained by it.

—Hebrews 12:10, 11

Protection

A father is
    instinctively protective
        of his children.

    He provides
        a firm grasp
            on the hand of his toddler,
            crossing a busy street;
        a watchful eye
            on the growing child,
            testing his boundaries;
        a word of
            wisdom, guidance, or warning
            to the fledgling
                asserting his independence.

Protective measures
    of a loving father!

Our Heavenly Father
    also protects his children.

    His firm grasp
        will guide you
            through the busy highways
            of life.
    He watches protectively
        as his growing child
            tests the boundaries
            of his love.
    His word provides
        wisdom, guidance, and warning
            to his child
            seeking identity and direction.

Protective measures
    of a loving father!

The eyes of the LORD
   are on those who fear him,
   on those whose hope
      is in his unfailing love.

—Psalm 33:18

The LORD delights
   in the way of the man
   whose steps he has made firm;
though he stumble,
   he will not fall,
   for the LORD upholds him
      with his hand.

—Psalm 37:23, 24

For the eyes of the LORD
   range throughout the earth
   to strengthen those
      whose hearts
      are fully committed to him.

—2 Chronicles 16:9

Father - Child Relationships

Among the treasures of fatherhood
    are shared moments of accomplishment
        with your child—
    times when your child
        follows the right path
            and makes you proud—SUCCESS!

There are other moments also—FAILURES!—
    times when your child
        wants to go his own way . . .
    moments marred by
        rebellion,
            wrong choices,
                disappointments.

How can you handle these times of
    strained relationship,
        disillusionment,
            anger?

At times such as these,
    your Heavenly Father's example
        can give you patience and courage
        to sustain you while you await
        the return of your wayward child.

And, he can help you maintain LOVE
    sufficient to greet your
        returning prodigal
        with open arms—
    just as the Father
        waits for YOU!

As a father has compassion
on his children,
so the LORD has compassion
on those who fear him.

—Psalm 103:13

Train a child
in the way he should go,
and when he is old
he will not turn from it.

—Proverbs 22:6

A fool gives full vent
to his anger,
but a wise man
keeps himself
under control.

Discipline your son,
and he will give you peace;
he will bring delight
to your soul.

—Proverbs 29:11, 17

Jesus said,
"See that you do not
look down
on one of these
little ones.

"Your Father in heaven
is not willing
that any of these
little ones
should be lost."

—Matthew 18:10, 14

Setting the Example

One of the greatest challenges,
for you as a father,
is setting the right example
for your children.

Children DO follow
the example
of their fathers.

How quickly those little ones
imitate your actions
and pick up your words—
good or bad.

How important, then,
if you would have
your child learn the way
of eternal life,
that you provide
a good example
both in word and deed.

What a priceless privilege it is
to introduce your youngster
to the Son of God,
Jesus Christ,
who was given by his Father
that we might enjoy
eternal life.

Be imitators of God, therefore,
as dearly loved children
and live a life of love,
just as Christ loved us
and gave himself up for us
as a fragrant offering
and sacrifice to God.

—Ephesians 5:1, 2

Jesus said,
"I have set you an example
that you should do
as I have done for you."

—John 13:15

Set an example . . .
in speech,
in life,
in love,
in faith, and
in purity.

—1 Timothy 4:12

O LORD, . . . your hand will guide me,
your right hand
will hold me fast.

—Psalm 139:1, 10

*That every man may eat and drink,
and find satisfaction in all his toil—
this is the gift of God.*

—Ecclesiastes 3:13

Making a Living

Whether it's called labor, job,
   employment, business, career,
   or simply—MAKING A LIVING—
work is a necessary and natural part
   of being a father.

Providing your family with
   food, shelter,
   clothing, and security
      is no simple task!

It takes much
   time, energy, and thought.

And sometimes,
   it is easy to fall
      into the trap
      of giving work
      too much of yourself.

However important your work is,
   it must be balanced
      with other things.

There must be
   time for your family and
   time for yourself,
   time for rest,
            recreation,
                  refreshment!

And, especially time
   to develop and strengthen
      your relationship
      with the Heavenly Father
      who wants you to enjoy
         the life he gave you.

Make it your ambition
　　to lead a quiet life,
　　to mind your own business, and
　　to work with your hands, . . .
so that your daily life
　　may win the respect of outsiders
　　and so that you will not be
　　　　dependent on anybody.

—1 Thessalonians 4:11, 12

A word from Jesus:

　"Do not worry, saying,
　　'What shall we eat?' or
　　'What shall we drink?' or
　　'What shall we wear?'
　For the pagans run after
　　all these things,
　　and your heavenly Father knows
　　　that you need them.
　But seek first his kingdom
　　and his righteousness,
　　and all these things
　　　will be given to you as well."

—Matthew 6:31-33

Financial Pressure

Utility payments,
   auto expenses,
      house repairs,
        doctor bills.
Is there no end to them?

Just about the time you think
   you are going to get out
      from under it all,
   something happens, and
the money-go-round begins again.

Perhaps you think
   the problems would be solved
      if only you had more money.
But would they?

It seems that even when
   there is more money,
there just never seems to be enough.

You have a Heavenly Father
     who is concerned about
   the financial pressure you feel.

The bills will probably keep coming,
   all earthly belongings
   may be lost,
   the pressure may continue,
     but rest assured—
God will always be with you.

Remember, your Heavenly Father knows
   all about those problems—
     those situations that test,
     develop, and expand your faith.

I know what it is
  to be in need,
and I know what it is
  to have plenty.

I have learned the secret
  of being content
  in any and every situation,
    whether well fed or hungry,
    whether living in plenty
      or in want.

I can do everything
  through him
    who gives me strength.

—Philippians 4:12, 13

God is able to make
    all grace abound to you,
  so that in all things
    at all times,
  having all that you need,
  you will abound
    in every good work.

He who supplies seed to the sower
    and bread for food
  will also supply and increase . . .
    the harvest
      of your righteousness.

—2 Corinthians 9:8, 10

Success

You work, you struggle, you sweat,
    and still you fail . . .

What is success?
    A new home?
        A new boat?
            A new car?

There is certainly
    nothing wrong with these.

But if success is measured
    by these possessions,
then success, at best,
    would be temporary.

God's Word reveals
    how we can be successful—
with, or without, possessions.

True success is not measured
    by what you *have*
but by what you *are*.
And *what* you are is determined
    by *whose* you are.

Work at developing
    your relationship with God.

Spend time with his Word:
    Commit it to memory.
    Meditate on its teachings
        so that your children
        will desire to follow
            your godly way of life.

Be successful . . . God's way!

"Do not store up for yourselves
treasures on earth,
where moth and rust destroy,
and where thieves break in
and steal.
But store up for yourselves
treasures in heaven, . . .
For where your treasure is,
there your heart will be also."

—Matthew 6:19-21

Better a little
with the fear of the LORD
than great wealth with turmoil!

—Proverbs 15:16

When God gives any man
wealth and possessions,
and enables him to enjoy them,
to accept his lot
and be happy in his work—
this is a gift of God.

—Ecclesiastes 5:19

He who pursues
righteousness and love,
finds life, prosperity and honor.

—Proverbs 21:21

A Father's Prayers

Powerful, indeed, is the effect
   of a father's prayers
      on behalf of his children!

What a sense of security is provided
      for the child who knows that
   Dad is sufficiently concerned
      to talk daily with the Lord
      about his or her welfare.

Prayer not only transfers the burden
   from the father and child
      to the Lord,
   but it establishes a rapport
      between them.

And when the answers come,
   times of rejoicing and celebration
      become a family affair.

That wonderful feeling of fulfillment
      is experienced
   when the desires of your heart
      have been granted!

What a privilege can be yours,
      through the family's
      daily devotional time,
   to weave into the fabric
      of your children's lives
      the knowledge that
God has a plan for each of their lives.

The prayer of a righteous man
  is powerful and effective.

                    —James 5:16

Do not be anxious about anything,
  but in everything,
  by prayer and petition,
    with thanksgiving,
  present your requests to God.
And the peace of God,
  which transcends all understanding,
  will guard your hearts
    and your minds
      in Christ Jesus.

                    —Philippians 4:6, 7

Beauty for Ashes

Perhaps as you look back
over your life,
you see many failures.

Your family life
has not been
what you had hoped.

Your children
have disappointed you.

Or, perhaps,
you have simply not met
your own expectations.

One of the best things
about your Heavenly Father
is that he is
a God of beginnings.

He will
forgive *and* forget
the past.

He will
give you joy and purpose
today.

And he will
lead you boldly into
tomorrow.

Trust the Lord to take you
from yesterday's failures
into tomorrow's victories!

Blessed is he
  whose transgressions
    are forgiven,
  whose sins are covered.

Blessed is the man
  whose sin
  the LORD does not count
    against him
  and in whose spirit
    there is no deceit.

—Psalm 32:1, 2

There is now
  no condemnation
  for those who are
    in Christ Jesus.

—Romans 8:1

Trust in the LORD
    with all your heart
  and lean not
    on your own understanding;
  in all your ways
    acknowledge him,
  and he will make
    your paths straight.

—Proverbs 3:5, 6

Costly Commitment

When the bills started coming in,
   you probably realized
      that having a family
      was going to be
         a costly commitment.

Those financial obligations
   are only the beginning
   of a father's investment
      in the life
      of his beloved child.

It seems like a lot to ask
   of a father,
      doesn't it?

Yet, a loving father
   willingly pays the price.

The Heavenly Father
   also counted the cost
      of providing believers
      with membership
         in his family.

He willingly paid the price—
   the death of his
      only begotten Son.

It seems like a lot to ask
   of a Heavenly Father,
      doesn't it?

But, our loving Father
   willingly paid the price!

Because of his great love for us,
  God, who is rich in mercy,
    made us alive with Christ
    even when we were dead
      in transgressions—
  it is by grace
  you have been saved.

—Ephesians 2:4, 5

What, then, shall we say
  in response to this?
If God is for us,
  who can be against us?
He who did not spare
  his own Son,
  but gave him up for us all—
  how will he not also,
    along with him,
  graciously give us
    all things?

—Romans 8:31, 32

He [Jesus] was pierced
  for our transgressions,
He was crushed
  for our iniquities;
the punishment that brought us peace
  was upon him,
and by his wounds
  we are healed.

—Isaiah 53:5

A Father's Love

A loving father works hard
   to provide for his family.

Providing for the present
   with an eye toward the future,
     he wants for them
       only the best.

God also wants
   only the very best
     for his children.

With a protective hand
   on your present
and an eye toward
   your eternal future,
God provided
   the very best for you.

Acting according to
   his Father's will,
Jesus took upon himself
   the sins of all
     who would trust in him.

The Son of God died on the cross
   and then rose from the grave,
     so that all who believe
     might be provided
       with the best!

Forgiveness!
   Peace!
     Joy!
       Eternal Life!

Provisions of a loving Father.

My God will meet
all your needs
according to
his glorious riches
in Christ Jesus.

—Philippians 4:19

For God so loved the world
that he gave
his one and only Son,
that whoever
believes in him
shall not perish
but have eternal life.

—John 3:16

Praise be to
the God and Father
of our Lord Jesus Christ!
In his great mercy
he has given us
new birth
into a living hope
through the resurrection
of Jesus Christ
from the dead.

—1 Peter 1:3

A Father's Decision

Perhaps after sharing
these thoughts,
you have found yourself
growing closer
to the Heavenly Father
with whom you have already
established a relationship.

Or, maybe, you have come
to a realization
that you do not yet have
this close personal tie
with the Heavenly Father.

You can know him!
Not just as a God
way up there,
but, as a Father, who wants
a close, caring,
personal relationship
with you as his child.

You commit your life to him
as his child.

He commits himself to you
as your Father.

There are responsibilities,
but the joys are unlimited!

You can establish
such a relationship
by praying the prayer,
on the opposite page,
that will help you express
this desire of your heart.

Dear God,

I confess that I am a sinner,
unworthy of your love.
Please forgive my sins
and come into my heart,
cleansing my life
from all sinfulness.

I believe that your Son, Jesus,
died on the cross for my sin
and that he rose again
so I might have eternal life.

I need your forgiveness of my sins,
your cleansing,
your love,
your wisdom,
that I may become
a godly father—
one who is pleasing to you.

I want you to become
the Lord and Master of my life
and to help me guide my family
in the pathway that leads
to eternal life.

Thank you for being my Father
and for the privilege
of being a father myself.

I pray this in Jesus' name
and for his sake. Amen.

This booklet has been given to you by:

If you would like to have further help
in learning how to live
and walk with God,
please write us or call us.

We will be happy to help you!